The Colours We Eat

Odd One Out

Patricia Whitehouse

www.raintreepublishers.co.uk
Visit our website to find out more information about **Raintree** books.

To order:
- ☎ Phone 44 (0) 1865 888112
- 🖹 Send a fax to 44 (0) 1865 314091
- 💻 Visit the Raintree Bookshop at **www.raintreepublishers.co.uk** to browse our catalogue and order online.

First published in Great Britain by Raintree, Halley Court, Jordan Hill, Oxford OX2 8EJ, part of Harcourt Education.
Raintree is a registered trademark of Harcourt Education Ltd.

Editorial: Nick Hunter and Diyan Leake
Design: Sue Emerson (HL-US) and Joanna Sapwell (www.tipani.co.uk)
Picture Research: Amor Montes de Oca (HL-US) and Maria Joannou
Production: Jonathan Smith

Originated by Dot Gradations
Printed and bound in China by South China Printing Company

ISBN 1 844 21610 1 (hardback)
07 06 05 04 03
10 9 8 7 6 5 4 3 2 1

ISBN 1 844 21617 9 (paperback)
08 07 06 05 04
10 9 8 7 6 5 4 3 2 1

British Library Cataloguing in Publication Data
Whitehouse, Patricia
Odd One Out
641.3
A full catalogue record for this book is available from the British Library.

Acknowledgements
The publishers would like to thank the following for permission to reproduce photographs: Fraser (Greg Beck) pp. **18**, **19**; Heinemann Library (Michael Brosilow) pp. **4**, **5**, **8**, **9**, **10**, **11**, **12**, **13**, 14, 15, 16, 17, 22, -**23**, back cover; Visuals Unlimited (Eric Anderson) pp. **3**, **6**, **7**, **20**, **21**.

Cover photograph of fruit and vegetables reproduced with permission of Popperfoto

Every effort has been made to contact copyright holders of any material reproduced in this book. Any omissions will be rectified in subsequent printings if notice is given to the publishers.

Which food is the odd one out?

Here are some foods, but something is wrong.

One food in this picture doesn't belong. (The green pepper)

What doesn't belong?

Here are some yellow foods, but something is wrong.

Which one of these foods doesn't belong?

The green kiwi fruit doesn't belong.

What doesn't belong?

Here are some green foods, but something is wrong.

Which one of these foods doesn't belong?

The red tomato doesn't belong.

What doesn't belong?

Here are some red foods, but something is wrong.

Which one of these foods doesn't belong?

The glass of white milk
doesn't belong.

What doesn't belong?

Here are some white foods, but something is wrong.

Which one of these foods doesn't belong?

The red soup doesn't belong.

What doesn't belong?

Here are some other red foods, but something is wrong.

Which of these foods doesn't belong?

The yellow **pineapple** doesn't belong.

What doesn't belong?

Here are some other yellow foods, but something is wrong.

Which one of these foods doesn't belong?

The green lettuce doesn't belong.

What doesn't belong?

Here are some big foods, but something is wrong.

Which of these foods don't belong?

The little red beans don't belong.

What doesn't belong?

Here are some small foods, but something is wrong.

Which one of these foods doesn't belong?

The big yellow banana
doesn't belong.

Which didn't belong?

Here are the foods that didn't belong.

This food is too good to last very long!

What belongs where?

What should go in the red basket?

What should go in the green basket?

Look for the answers on page 24.

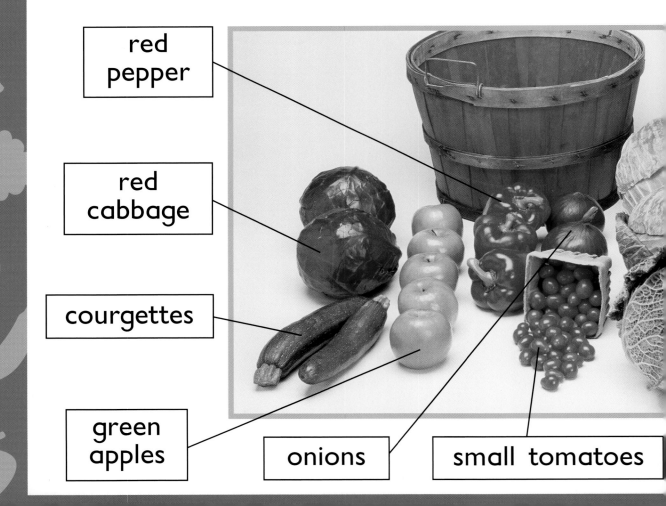

red pepper

red cabbage

courgettes

green apples

onions

small tomatoes

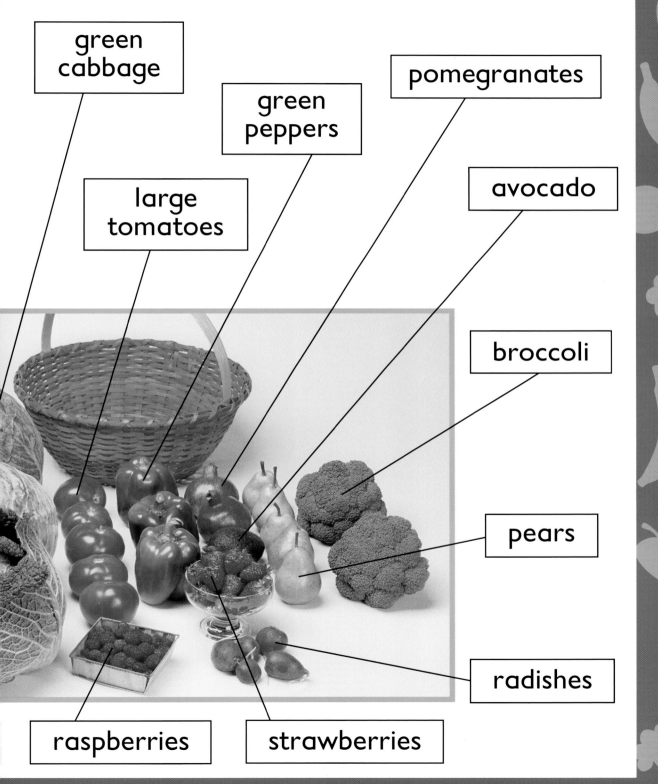

green
cabbage

green
peppers

pomegranates

large
tomatoes

avocado

broccoli

pears

radishes

raspberries

strawberries

23

Index

Answers to quiz on page 22

The red cabbages, red peppers, tomatoes, raspberries, red onions, pomegranates, strawberries and radishes go in the red basket.

The courgettes, green apples, green cabbages, green peppers, avocado, pears and broccoli go in the green basket.